Don't You Dare Teach My Daughter to Fear the Forest

& Other Poems of Remembrance for Women

★

by T.Y. Chambers

This book is an offering to the souls of all women

It reflects the journey of the author

Each woman's journey is unique

Every woman's journey is valid

Womanhood is a truth that lives in some indefinable

space within us

Although your own journey may not be perfectly

reflected

Please know

We see you

We honor your truth

And the divine sisterhood of our souls

Table of Contents

INTRODUCTION TO THE ARCHETYPES   6

THE MAIDEN   10

THE REALITY OF WOMAN   11

HOW TO TRANSLATE FOR THE GODDESS   15

WHO I AM   20

THE MOTHER   25

DON'T YOU DARE TEACH MY DAUGHTER TO FEAR THE FOREST   26

THE WOUNDS OF THE MOTHER   32

THE RECLAMATION OF THE CROWN   39

THE ENCHANTRESS   44

LESSONS IN LETTING GO   45

THE SPIRITUAL QUEST   50

THE PRIESTESS LIVES ON   57

THE CRONE   61

THE POEM WOMEN WHISPER AT MIDNIGHT   62

THE WISE WOMAN KNOWS   66

YOU ARE MY LIGHT   69

THE WISDOM OF THE CRONE   72

ABOUT THE AUTHOR   75

ARTWORK CREDITS   77

Introduction to the Archetypes

The female menstrual cycle has four distinct phases that menstruating women flow through every month and which anciently correspond with the phases of the Moon. These phases have long been associated with four female archetypes:

Maiden/Virgin
Mother
Enchantress/Wild Woman
Crone/Wise Woman

Women can embody these archetypes every single day, through each menstrual cycle and/or lunar month, and throughout their entire life.

During our busy lives it is easy not to incorporate this, and to completely miss the essential, changing faces of femininity that connect us to who we truly are. But by embracing the emergence of these archetypes each day, each month, and throughout our lives, we get to celebrate these aspects of ourselves instead of fearing, ignoring, or repressing them.

The energy of these archetypes can be harnessed and utilised to their full potential when we recognise them. The following are examples of how and when these energies might emerge in you.

Maiden / waxing crescent moon / pre-
ovulation

This archetype embodies independence and so answers to no one. She emerges to remind you of the power you possess to co-create with the Divine.

The Maiden brings purity of mind and of heart, as well as the need for freedom.

Mother / full moon / ovulation

The mother archetype encompasses sacred care-taking and the instinct to nurture rather than control. It is the ability to foster growth, and then let go.

The Mother is aware of the part she plays in the cycle of nature. With her you feel the need to be closer to the Earth and you hear the land calling you home much clearer than in any other phase.

```
Enchantress / wild woman / waning
full moon / pre-menstrual phase
```

This phase is often associated with physical and mental pain. It is here that your grief asks to be healed and integrated, and it is your inner wild woman whom answers the call. She is also known as Shaman, medicine woman, healer. This archetype is 'wild' because she needs to be in order to connect with the otherworldly aspects of existence: to sense, intuit, and feel pain in all its forms, as opposed to simply the surface symptoms.

Crone / wise woman / dark moon /
bleeding time

The presence of the Crone marks your transition
from the energy of the Enchantress. It is through
her that the darkness and the wild, deep emotions
felt during the previous phase are transmuted into
wisdom. She embodies the lessons taught in
previous phases; her job is to reveal the true
nature of your soul, to create the conditions
necessary for renewal and rebirth in your life.

★

The Maiden

The Reality of Woman

It has been said that women have expected roles

and duties that if fulfilled,

make us

real

women.

And if a woman can be categorized under one

label, she is a

real

woman.

But if she decides to be something else

She is an unstable woman

a confusing

too bold

too daring woman.

Too risky

too deep

too little woman.

A woman who has had the courage to step out of her box will be told to

get right back in: "You've had your fun, don't make a fuss."

But it's too late

It's too late because I've taken a match to that damn box:

my wings,

seared from the cremation of my fears into ashes.

Now I've cut water on the backs of blue whales

I can't go back.

I've braved heights with the beat of eagle feathers beneath me

So I can't go back.

They had hoped that the box would contain me, not knowing that I would find

my voice in silence, that I would discover my light in the dark.

No! I won't go back.

Instead I create in the stillness of night

And birth newer versions of myself

Each wiser than the last

Baptized by ocean spray, under a full moon.

I am reborn.

★

Affirmation

I cannot be contained

I cannot be tamed

My voice

My body

My heart

Are wild and free

How to Translate for the Goddess

I'm a weary translator for the Goddess

trying to envision all the ways

sacred ideas

which are always expressed in the masculine

might apply to me

Like a gymnast in a double layout full out

my thoughts twist and turn

flip 'God' backwards and forwards

The 'He's'

And the 'brotherhood'

And the 'son'

And the 'father'

All thrown about as if we were on stage in a ballet

Strewn out like clothes on a busy changing room
floor

Too small

Too big

How on earth can I get these to fit?

Each word, a shard of glass from a broken mirror

In which one can I see myself?

Tossed like a salad

Which word tastes the most like 'woman'?

I am a weary translator for the Goddess

drinking in the masculine

and drowning in it

Until the feminine is expelled

from my body, mind, and soul in a cleansing

A watery exorcism

A dispelling of the truth of me

My interpretation of the sacred

My experience with the divine

How many times have you tried to rise up in a search
for the sacred

only to be forced upon your knees

and told that the journey has already been made

by a man. That you need search no more?

For a person with no experience is but a child

And we women have been kept as daughters

Excluded from our sacred womanhood

by the ancient power of words

that have scratched and scraped our skin

and decorated our souls in open sores

I'm a weary healer for the Goddess

Attempting to heal these wounds

Passed down to me from my mother's mother.

But I heal because I have found the cure

It is to seek spiritual experience and interpret it
for myself.

Through art

Through writing

Through dance

Through music and journeying

Through knowing and understanding the inner
workings of my own body

Through accepting every flaw

And through my raw heart

To stand in our womanhood

That is the cure

★

Affirmation

Within all that I do
Lies my healing

I will choose
How I think
How I feel
How I act
With
Wisdom

Who I Am

I feel like I've spent my whole life trying to show
you who I am

But you can't see me, dear friend

You just won't see me

You have ideas of who you want me to be

And there are those visions of who I should be that
leave my colour smudged

and my shine dulled

Do I conform and die?

Live and lie?

You don't want to see me

One evening I journeyed to the desert

to ask the Goddess what I should do

My dress scraped the sand,

grains between my toes

And I was just about to give up and go home

when a glimmer of sun shone out from behind the
dusty mountains.

It lit up my heart, and moved my soul, and I heard
the words,

"You were created in the spirit of 'be'"

I felt the sacred drum

and my wild heart was loosened

by the Deep Feminine's song.

I had my bright night of the soul and I was going to

Be

In the desert is where I saw myself for who I am

But you, dear friend

You can't see me

You say

I love too hard, that I love too soft, that I need too
fiercely after only one night

But a lunar eclipse has an evening to complete

And a meteoroid needs only a second to fall

A cloud takes an instant to burst

A thousand stars can die in a minute...

I am reflected in them, but you can't see me

You say I'm too emotional, too feeling-full, too 'woman'

But who can stand the weight of mountains and not sink back into the soft, grassy Earth but a little?

You say it is because I am weak that I lie here on the ground, my tears wetting the soil.

I say it is because *I am* the Earth, and that sometimes us women get called

Home

To water baby seeds

To grow new life...

So, dear friend

I vow to stop wishing you would change your mind

about who you think I should

Be

If I can be found in the Earth and sky,

then so can you

And if I can accept me,

then so can you

And if I can see beauty in myself,

then so can you

For I have learnt that I can't *make* anyone *see*

All I can do is show *you* who *you* are

just by being me.

★

Affirmation

There is a wise woman within

Who is my true mirror

She defines her boundaries

She is the essence of bliss

I invite her to make herself known to me today.

I am listening

The Mother

Don't You Dare Teach My Daughter to Fear the Forest

Don't you dare teach my daughter to be afraid of
the forest

This is how you have created the fear of the search
within

I never want my daughter to limit her journey to
bright, open places

places that are easy to touch and see

I have learned that sometimes the truth of who we
are lies in shadows and damp places, where
mushrooms grow and plants reach out sideways,
down-ways and new-ways, haphazardly searching
for sun.

It is my own journey that taught me this,

that women come into this world with a forest

ancient, jagged, and wise – a forest nestled deep inside our souls. So, you can try to scare my daughter out of the forest

but I am going to tell her

about her ability to lay roots and to respect the roots of others

That these are her veins, her connection to love, to the Divine,

her roots back to herself. I am going to teach her that her heart-roots ground her, that green is the colour of love.

My daughter will know that things are allowed to birth and grow wild inside her soul-forest: ideas, thoughts, secrets, intuitions – but that they may die in winter, when they have broken free and had their day in the sun.

And when mistakes have been made and she realises that she has taken the wrong forest path for her, I will teach my daughter to look to the moon for the way back home

And my daughter will know that her soul-forest is there for her to retreat to, that she will find true abundance, true nourishment, and true peace, that it holds the mystery to the meaning of life

The shadows are there to make the journey to uncovering that mystery all the more exciting. If the time ever comes when my daughter should feel that life has worn her down, I will show her that in the soul-forest there is always life teeming under the surface -

Jewel-green grasshoppers and velvet-winged butterflies in a never-ending dance to the Earth's song.

So don't you dare teach my daughter to fear the forest.

You know those stories that speak of the wolf in the wood?

I will teach my daughter that she is the wolf –

free, primal, and connected to the moon

And you know those wicked witches in crooked cottages hidden behind dark oaks?

I will let my daughter know that she is the witch

She is the wise woman who lives in her own soul-forest I will tell her that the witch is the crone, her elder, her wisdom;

the dark moon in all her glory

There is no dark mystery that you can scare my daughter with because I am going to teach her that she is at the heart of that mystery

My daughter will know that her divine, feminine power is the greatest enigma of all to those who don't understand

Women will not fear our own innate power

and we are rising to howl, "*No more*".

So don't you dare teach our daughters to fear the forest

No more.

★

Affirmation

There is nothing to fear from looking within

I am the wicked witch
I am the moon
I am the shadow
I am the wolf

I will not fracture myself in denial of all that I am.

All the answers I seek live in the dark as well as the light

The Wounds of the Mother

They say I have my mother's eyes. They shine an
English hazel when I rim them with Kohl

In honour of my Turkish ancestors

Strong women with strong arms sporting rolled up
sleeves

ready to pound dough into flat bread to feed their
children

They say I have inherited her power of spirit

her quiet voice

the un-elegant way she expresses her emotions

"You are just like her!" they cry in delight

And I smile

My wonderful, ever-giving mother is just like me

But then I realised that nobody ever told me I had inherited her wounds

Deep, dark holes in the ground. Tunnels that lead far away from the light, wounds that feel like shards of

broken glass

broken dreams

broken expectations

that pierce the soul and deflate it

in a way that only disappointment can

So, one clear day

I surrendered and sat with them

I melted myself down

and became one with them

Loosened them from my belief that they were
invaders of my spirit

And listened to them

sing their wisdom

Heavy

Like cascading water off a mountainside

"The tears you cry are not your own"

"The river you cry cannot be made alone"

"It is made from the tears of your mother's mother's
mother's mother as this

river runs deep and far back."

So I knelt down beside this river and I watched as the tears from my eyes dripped into the duck-egg blue water and snaked away.

I heard her message in her curves and the way she moved

like velvet, over and through all obstacles in her path

She said,

"Every woman who heals herself, heals all the women who came before her and all the women who come after her,"

And

at last

I understood

So I stood up, open to changing my mind about the world and proclaimed that I didn't want the sadness of women to continue. I didn't want to watch them sacrifice, bow down, or martyr themselves any more in the name of love.

I chanted over and over to the sky

to the Goddess

to myself

that I will heal

because I would never want my daughters to cry my tears

So, when my mother is sad

 I heal myself

When my sisters are sad

I heal myself

When I read stories of women around the world
who are victims of violence

I heal myself

When a friend makes a choice she later regrets

I heal myself

When I think of my grandmother's difficult life

I heal myself

Because in my healing, I reach out and heal with
every woman who ever graced this Earth

And every woman yet to walk it

★

Affirmation

I am a catalyst for change

I inspire healing in others

By healing myself

The Reclamation of the Crown

Oh my beautiful sisters!

Don't you know it's okay to bow your head to receive your crown?

The way the Great Mother releases summer every year and welcomes death

Let go

Let in

Let out

Know yourself and meet your queen-self. She calls to you to

Stop

Breathe

Feel the heaviness

That's right. Feel it.

There, on your right shoulder is the weight of that mistake you made

There, on the other, is the burden of that loved one you think you've failed

The crushing on your back is that relationship you just couldn't get to run right

Oh! How you tried! How you loved! How you burned!

I Stop

I Breathe

I Feel

and the pain of it pierces my chest

the guilt of it squeezes my heart

My hand reaches over my left breast

as if I have the power to heal with an open palm

I hang my head and my hair falls forward, tickling my chin

I stay like that for what feels like forever as I silently travel back in time

And it is in that silence that I hear a voice

Her voice that can only be heard in rain storms and tsunamis and forest fires

She simply says,

Rise

And so, my spine realigns as my chin leads the way, and I rise

Rise, because life goes on

Rise, because you are free

Rise, because you have done your best

Rise, because you have loved like ocean waves

Rise, in the knowing that there is no shame in bowing to pain

because in rising you do no less than reclaim your queen-hood

And you will rise again

Wiser and wilder than before

Oh! my dearest sister

Don't you know it's okay to bow your head to receive your crown?

★

Affirmation

In my failure and my mistakes

I know that I have the opportunity to rise from them

Wilder than before

Although my hair is matted

And I have mud on my paws

The emeralds in my crown still glitter

With the strength of me

Today is the day I reclaim my queen-hood

The Enchantress

Lessons in letting go

My spiritual path is my own.

It is called the-way-of-the-one-who-lets-go

There's only one rule on this path

And it is that you

Release

Relinquish

Let go

Let live

And let die

I know now

when to give up

For I have lived wild like the wind

and I have fallen like the rain

and I have burned with the sun

I've grown roots as yew trees grow roots

Desperate and unruly, but with a target in mind

Blind

I've felt around in darkness

under the cold Earth

and in places where it is too lonely to breed love

But burn I did anyway

and twirled roots around dead things

and brought them up to the surface, too afraid to
let go, until I realized that holding on wouldn't
rouse him from his deep sleep and squeezing him
tighter wouldn't make him wake.

For he is dozing in his peaceful slumber

and my burning sun

can't touch him.

My cries on the wind

are muffled to his ears.

You said it was unnatural

dear sister

for him not to love you back

For him not to comfort you in your hour of need,

that it was unnatural to have such a lack of
compassion as he showed you time and time again.

But what is more unnatural?

For a cherry tree to retain its blossoms in a
hurricane?

Or a leaf to stay green in a snow storm?

Or an apple to cling to its branch

and ignore the voice calling it home?

Things die sister

Things die

And some things never grow to begin with

So remember the wise Earth

blessed one

and welcome the winter

Because you deserve to live wild

like the wind

★

Affirmation

I embrace change
I allow nature to take her course

I know when to let go

Nothing outside myself is guaranteed to stay with
me forever
So I look to the Divine for stability

She is my security
Through all hardships
and for that I am grateful

The Spiritual Quest

I've travelled the world

searching for items for my sacred altar

A slab of worn wood

paint peeled back

placed in the corner of the room

A reminder to pray

A mirror to my soul

Take me back home to God

Meticulously placed beeswax candles resting in
the four corners

A scattering of Turkish rose petals

An English yew tree branch

An autumnal cluster of leaves

Our Lady, calmly standing amidst the chaos

Arms outstretched in surrender

Yes

Here was my holy altar

But then I fell in love

and I discovered my moon-like heart

which waxed and waned
And when I experienced the dark,

prayer was my light,

Palms touching was my way back home,

The bow of my head was my surrender,

My knees on the ground

my truth

And so all the candles

And leaves

And roses

Fell away

until it was just me kneeling there

And it was then I learnt

that my heart is my altar

And in my search for God

I looked for sacred space

A place where the Divine speaks its

drop-to-your-knees

throw-your-hands-up

truth

Where I could dance between ancient oaks

And pray on mountaintops

And draw the Goddess down

But then my niece was born into this world

And her holiness was evident in her every breath

Her divinity pervading her every glance

Her Godliness

still in her touch and her smell

She had been created in sacredness

A literal sanctity that is the womb

I knew I had found my sacred space within me

So then I searched for The Word

A snippet of wisdom that would remind me of
home

A map that would guide me back to where I had
come from

A holy story

to connect me to God

Until one day I decided to read my heart

And listen to the rush of the blood through my
veins

Sometimes, I was soaring over ancient Palmyra

and breathing in the fresh scent of Damascene
jasmine

Sometimes I was underground,

so alone with what I had done that my memories
seeped into my flesh

And my regrets burned into my muscle

Until I realized my story had been written on my
bones

And it is this story that is now my holy book

Its words

The Words of wisdom I spent so long looking for

I have given my whole life to my search for
the sacred

And discovered myself.

My body is the temple

my altar stands within

My womb is my sacred space
The words on my bones

are the words of God

And the wisdom they contain

is my own

Here is the sacred woman

and this is the truth of her

So to you sister

I bow

★

Affirmation

There is nothing I can search for

That does not already exist within me.

I am a vessel for the Divine

The Priestess Lives On

They say that the role of the priestess in modern
society has been buried

Like a crumbling temple left to decay under sand

Regarded unimportant by the men who determine

What society should

embrace

remember

and hold dear

They don't know that the priestess lives on.

How many times have you assured a friend that
they are good enough?

And in how many ways have you given someone
space to fall?

Have you ever given someone time to show you
who they truly are?

Even when they were not sure themselves?

And so the priestess lives on

Can you remember a time when you witnessed a person kick away their tight

bud?

Burst into blossom?

Embrace the sky?

And so the priestess lives on

And when was the last time you kissed someone goodbye?

Leaving the wet of your lips on their cheeks,

like holy water on foreheads,

like rain on cracked Earth.

And so the priestess lives on

To witness

Hold space

Bless

And heal

This is the work of the priestess

So in you,

The priestess lives on

★

Affirmation

I carry out the work of a priestess in my daily life

I am at the service of the Divine

So I ask Her:

What would you have me do today?

What would you have me say?

Where would you have me go?

The Crone

The Poem Women Whisper At Midnight

It has been said that women are the weaker sex,
That our dispositions more prone to mental and
emotional instability,
That our wombs are the source of all that is wrong
with the world.
The term hysteria comes from the Greek
word *hysterika*, meaning Uterus.

They claim that they can see the woman in the Earth
And that, men are in the sun
And that she grows new life at the mere touch of his
yellow fingers,
So he has the right to claim it.

Woman is the empty vessel that needs filling,
That is all they say we are.
Fill our wombs,
Our minds with who you think we should be,
Our mouths with what you think we should speak.

They say that when we menstruate we are dirty

That after we give birth we are unclean,

Placenta and blood.

Hide them away like they don't exist.

And woman shouldn't have sex or she is tainted,

Woman shouldn't not have sex or she is broken.

Being a woman is dirty,

Unclean,

Tainted,

Broken.

It is said that women are afraid of nature,

That we fear the wolves that guard the city walls,

That if we walk far enough into the forest we will get

lost.

Because wildness is unbecoming in a woman.

How will she ever find a husband?

It is believed that women are the carriers of original

sin,

That we brought evil into the world,

That we can corrupt the greatest of men,

That our power is insidious, hideous, downright bad.

Well let me tell you what it is that is said also.

It is said that people fear what they do not
understand,

It is believed that people will attack,

What they think has a power greater than their own,

That the oppressor will do anything to suppress an
uprising,

That if you have to lay down the law with violence,

You were never in charge to begin with.

★

Affirmation

Oppression can take place in the mind and collective
unconscious as well as in the physical world.
Therefore…

"I loosen myself from all beliefs, past and present,
That block me from reaching my full potential as a
woman.

This is a prayer
For my sisters and I
That we may not forget the truth of ourselves today."

The Wise Woman Knows

We are inside all that there is and all that ever will
be

We are women

constantly recreating versions of ourselves by the
light of the moon

Waxing, full, and waning

Maiden, Mother, Crone

We have been led to believe that we can only be
one or the other at any given time

But the wise woman knows

We are all three

At all times

We are potential

We are the present moment

We weave visions of the future into blankets we
lay over our loved ones

Like Russian nesting dolls

Under one layer of our woman lies another

whose faults and mistakes helped build a stronger
version of ourselves

Never forgotten

The wisdom of women past

live on inside us

Mother, Maiden, Crone

We are all three

At all times

Always

The wise woman knows

★

Affirmation

There is no moment in time that I have to wait for

I am everything I want to be

Right here

Right now

You Are My Light

I come to you, my moon,
 to make waves of the blood in my veins
so that I may find steadiness
on the seashore
where you and I are creating a life together.

I come to you, my sun
to grow the dark parts of me that have been
denied,
so that I may accept myself fully
so that the woman that I am
is not dismembered by society's obsession with
the light.

I come to you, my night sky
to crush stars into slivers of glass for me
so that I may make a mirror of remembrance
to never forget
the truth of myself.

Within you I have found my moon, my sun, the
stars and all my days.

Within you is the light I need on my journey to know myself.

★

Affirmation

I welcome people into my life

who remind me of my own sacredness

The Wisdom of the Crone

I am the queen of renovation

an architect with no fear of the storm

the shattering of my heart

a chance

to build new rooms

where more love can live

★

Affirmation

I have no fear of a broken heart

I always emerge from one

Wiser than before

Dedicated to my great grandmother, grandmother, mother, sisters, nieces, Julakha, Raluca, Eileen, Beth & of course my future daughter

About the Author

T.Y. Chambers is the number one bestselling Amazon author of 'The Truth of Love'. She currently resides in the Middle East, but originally hails from London, England. During the day Chambers teaches English, but at night she writes sacred feminine poetry by the light of the moon.

T.Y. Chambers believes in the healing power of women coming together and sharing, and so the words within this book are her sacred offering to you. Thank you for your support.

Follow T.Y. Chambers:

www.tychambers.co.uk

@thesacredfemininepoet (instagram)

@chambersty (facebook)

Artwork Credits

Editing, Offering to Women dedication, and

Affirmations design

by Elizabeth Comport.

Contact for editing and artwork:

Website: elizabethcomport.com

Book cover artwork

by Alice Mason.

Etsy Shop: AliceMasonArtist

Archetype illustrations

by Joan van der Wereld.

Contact for art commissions:

Joan.vanderwereld@gmail.com

Made in the USA
Monee, IL
27 December 2019